T0323697

Cambridge Elements ≡

Elements in Poetry and Poetics
edited by
Eric Falci
University of California, Berkeley

THERESA HAK KYUNG CHA
IN BLACK AND WHITE

Josephine Nock-Hee Park
University of Pennsylvania

CAMBRIDGE
UNIVERSITY PRESS

Shaftesbury Road, Cambridge CB2 8EA, United Kingdom

One Liberty Plaza, 20th Floor, New York, NY 10006, USA

477 Williamstown Road, Port Melbourne, VIC 3207, Australia

314–321, 3rd Floor, Plot 3, Splendor Forum, Jasola District Centre,
New Delhi – 110025, India

103 Penang Road, #05–06/07, Visioncrest Commercial, Singapore 238467

Cambridge University Press is part of Cambridge University Press & Assessment,
a department of the University of Cambridge.

We share the University's mission to contribute to society through the pursuit of
education, learning and research at the highest international levels of excellence.

www.cambridge.org
Information on this title: www.cambridge.org/9781009323437

DOI: 10.1017/9781009323451

First published 2023

A catalogue record for this publication is available from the British Library.

ISBN 978-1-009-32343-7 Paperback
ISSN 2752-5236 (online)
ISSN 2752-5228 (print)

Cambridge University Press & Assessment has no responsibility for the persistence
or accuracy of URLs for external or third-party internet websites referred to in this
publication and does not guarantee that any content on such websites is, or will
remain, accurate or appropriate.

Theresa Hak Kyung Cha in Black and White

Elements in Poetry and Poetics

DOI: 10.1017/9781009323451
First published online: August 2023

Josephine Nock-Hee Park
University of Pennsylvania

Author for correspondence: Josephine Nock-Hee Park,
jnpark3@english.upenn.edu

Abstract: *Theresa Hak Kyung Cha in Black and White* explores the relation between text, author, and reader – a nexus theorized as the "apparatus" in Cha's study of cinema – by tracing two key literary intertexts in *Dictée*: Henry James's "The Jolly Corner," a submerged literary resonance in *Apparatus*, Cha's anthology of film theory, and the writing of Saint Thérèse of Lisieux, a primary intertext at the heart of *Dictée*. In Cha's film theory, black and white is the flicker of the cinematic apparatus, and the Element's readings consider this contrasting palette in self-reflexive portraits in black and white. This Element reads flashes of identification, often in punishing self-encounters, and it dwells on the figure of the martyr to arrive at the death of Theresa Hak Kyung Cha, the patron saint of artists and scholars fascinated by her art and her suffering.

Keywords: Theresa Hak Kyung Cha, *Dictée*, Cathy Park Hong, *Apparatus*, Saint Thérèse of Lisieux

ISBNs: 9781009323437 (PB), 9781009323451 (OC)
ISSNs: 2752-5236 (online), 2752-5228 (print)

Contents

Introduction

Cathy Park Hong's 2020 *Minor Feelings: An Asian American Reckoning*, the signal elaboration of Asian American experience in our era, features a fresh inquiry into the circumstances of Theresa Hak Kyung Cha's death. Hong's focus on this tragedy is a return to the prophecy of Cha's final and total work of art, *Dictée*: Cha's death saturated my reading of *Dictée*, gave the book a haunted prophetic aura – *Dictée* is, after all, about young women who died violent deaths – although I would never admit to that interpretation in a class or a talk.[1]

In a chapter entitled "Portrait of the Artist," Hong tracks Cha's rape and murder in 1982, the year of *Dictée*'s publication. A detective on a cold case, Hong is both obsessive and rueful: "The younger version of me," she writes, "would have been annoyed that I'm now imposing a biographical reading onto *Dictée* as if her life were an answer key to a book that refuses answers" (171). The force of Hong's driving inquiry cuts against long-standing scholarly reticence around Cha's death – but what answers a biographical reading could offer for this work finally elude Hong's examination.

And so, though the chapter features gripping interviews with Cha's family and friends, the talk Hong has elicited does not broach *Dictée*'s refusals:

> Cha, I should note, developed an aesthetic out of silence, making it evident through her elisions that the English language is too meager and mediated a medium to capture the historical atrocities her people have endured. It was more truthful to have those horrors partially spoken, like Sapphic shrapnel, and ask the reader to imagine the unspeakable. In a way, the scholar is mirroring Cha's own rhetoric of silence. (165)

"Sapphic shrapnel": there is no better description of Cha's work. Though Hong does not pierce this "rhetoric of silence," her labors provide a startling portrait of the artist, and *Minor Feelings* as a whole is a study of artists: Cha emerges anew in Hong's interviews, and Hong's first-person identification with her predecessor produces a feeling lineage of avant-garde Asian American women artists. In thus resituating Cha, Hong fills in her portrait: "I'm imposing myself onto her, filling her in with myself" (171).

I offer a further imposition that aligns Cha's brutal extinction to her masterwork. Hong's obsessive return to Cha's death lays bare a simple but troubling truth: our knowledge of Cha's rape and murder conditions our reading of *Dictée*. Hong recalls her prior treatment of Cha's violent end: "Didn't I also type and then delete the word *rape* before *murder* when I wrote the review where I mentioned

---

[1] Cathy Park Hong, *Minor Feelings: An Asian American Reckoning* (New York: One World – Random House, 2020), 155. Subsequent page numbers in parentheses.

Cha?" Hong continues, "*Rape* burns a hole in the article and capsizes any argument" (172, original italics). The fact of rape cordoned off Cha's fate from appreciations of her art, and thus absented, a silence has settled around Theresa Hak Kyung Cha, even as her work has acquired increasing prominence. Hong has voiced the heretofore unspeakable resonances between the violent deaths enshrined in Cha's final work and her own, final suffering. In acknowledging this continuum, I propose to identify Cha's agony within her art.

Dictée is a book about the interaction of an artist with her materials and her readers – and yet, as Hong's searing interrogation reveals, we have come to read Cha's book without her. My reading is governed by Cathy Park Hong's longing to know Theresa Hak Kyung Cha, and I have returned to *Dictée* to find her for myself. This Element works through the relation between text, author, and reader – a nexus theorized as the "apparatus" in Cha's study of cinema – at the core of *Dictée*, and it follows her lead across the pages of her epic. With Cha as my guide, I work through two key intertexts in her work: an excerpt from Henry James's "The Jolly Corner," a submerged literary resonance in *Apparatus*, the anthology of film theory Cha assembled, and the writing of Saint Thérèse of Lisieux, a primary intertext in "Erato / Love Poetry," the cinematic core of *Dictée*. In thus tracing a literary thread lodged within her cinematic praxis into the story of a modern saint – and Cha's namesake – who binds rapture to torment, this study explores identificatory practices that materialize the artist.

Following Cha's clues, I pick my way across a black-and-white landscape: the cinematic apparatus that interlaces artist to viewer in black and white, the textual reproductions that disintegrate into black-and-white grains, and, ultimately, the black and white of sins and saints. *Theresa Hak Kyung Cha in Black and White* reads flashes of identification, often in punishing self-encounters, ultimately tracing these labors to Cha's death through the figure of the martyr. Theresa Hak Kyung Cha is the patron saint of growing generations of artists and scholars fascinated by her art and her suffering. This Element is an effort to locate the martyred artist within the shards of her art.

Black and White

One year before *Dictée*, Cha published *Apparatus*, a volume "conceived as a collection of Autonomous Works on the apparatus of cinema." *Apparatus* is an artifact of Cha's residence in Paris in the late 1970s, where she studied with theorists and practitioners of cinema – and reopening it, the redolence of its era is overpowering. Perceptive scholars of Cha have marked the salience of this collection for *Dictée*: *Apparatus* maps out Cha's theoretical milieu in the period of *Dictée*'s gestation.[2] The anthology opens with Cha's definition of the cinematic apparatus as "the interdependent operations comprising the 'film, the author of the film, the spectator'"; the cinematic apparatus is "the process of film," which Cha aims to reveal in her assemblage of "the theoretical writings and materials of filmmakers."[3]

Three essays by Jean-Louis Baudry form the theoretical spine of the collection, in which Baudry ponders the identificatory processes of cinema. It is the spectator, pitched within Plato's cave and steeped in Freudian dreamwork, who occupies pride of place in these discussions: the spectator, like the dreamer, has a participatory role in the "more-than-the-real" encountered on the screen.[4] "The entire cinematographic apparatus is activated in order to provoke this simulation," Baudry writes, explaining that "it is indeed a simulation of the condition of the subject" in which, ultimately, the subject "is led to produce mechanisms mimicking, simulating the apparatus which is no other than himself."[5] The technical cinematic apparatus plunged within the dreamer's psyche: this is how film theory went then, and it is also how Cha understood the profound interdependence that would animate her epic.

Marc Vernet's essay in the collection, "Blinking, Flickering, and Flashing of the Black-and-White Film," offers a visible means of registering these submerged operations: "black-and-white" (Vernet underscores his hyphenation "because it is not so much a question of their opposition as it is of their conjunction, their fusion") is "the representative, in the diegesis, of the enigma structure, of the fetishist economy, and of the cinematic apparatus."[6] "Black-and-white" marks a point of convergence between the story on screen – the diegesis – and how cinema functions – its apparatus; it is "none other than cinematic representation itself, none other than the uncertain status of the moving perspective image."[7] This "blinking, flickering, and flashing" registers Baudry's unconscious identificatory processes, and in Cha's hands, this trace of the apparatus flickers across multiple art forms. Black and white is the process of making art rendered visible in the unfolding work of art, and it is the palette for all of Theresa Hak Kyung Cha's works, whether filmic, performative, or poetic.

---

[2] Sue J. Kim's "*Apparatus*: Theresa Hak Kyung Cha and the Politics of Form," *Journal of Asian American Studies* 8.2 (2005): 143–169, situates *Apparatus* as a means of historicizing Cha's use of form. Kim indicts the abstraction and ultimate passivity of the volume, in which she identifies an "increasing reification of form" (146).

[3] From Cha's unpaginated preface to *Apparatus. Cinematographic Apparatus: Selected Writings*. New York: Tanam Press, 1981.

[4] Jean-Louis Baudry, "The Apparatus," in *Apparatus*, 41–62, at 41.   [5] Ibid., 61.

[6] Marc Vernet, "Blinking, Flickering, and Flashing of the Black-and-White Film," in *Apparatus*, 357–369, at 357, 365.

[7] Ibid., 365.

Roland Barthes's "Upon Leaving the Movie Theater," the opening contribution in *Apparatus*, marks a direct resonance with *Dictée*. "The subject who speaks here must admit one thing," begins the essay, "he loves leaving a movie theater." Barthes's leaving reads like a reverse instigation for *Dictée*'s "She is entering now," when Cha's text presents movements into the theater and onto the screen. The phenomenological bent of Barthes's departure ("He is stiff, a little numb, bundled up, chilly") resonates with the embodied experiences Cha details, but in the theater, the reverie Barthes describes is utterly different.[8] He is captivated by the image: "I glue my nose, to the point of disjointing it, on the mirror of the screen, to the imaginary other with which I identify myself narcissistically."[9] From this attachment, Barthes asks, "How does one pry oneself from the mirror?" to conclude "there is another way of going to the cinema": by becoming "two bodies at once," both the narcissistic self and a secondary one attuned to the situation of the theater.[10] Barthes is careful to stipulate that this secondary position is not an intellectual one: "It is, so to speak, an amorous distance."[11] The fascination of this distance offers another mode of pleasure.

The privilege of this doubled identification is unimaginable for Cha, whose "subject who speaks" is itself uncertain. *Dictée*'s speaker, its "diseuse," suffers *"the pain of speech the pain to say"* (3); unlike Barthes's pleasurable bodies, she takes in others at the expense of her own integrity. Thy Phu's 2005 consideration of *Dictée*'s "decapitated forms" – citing a phrase from the "Clio / History" section of the text – positions Cha against "Barthes's self-absorption" by examining Cha's self-documentation. As Phu puts it, *Dictée* "is remarkable for its defacement and arguable erasure of the autobiographical 'I,'" illustrated by Cha's choice of photocopies over photographs of her family.[12] The black and white of the photocopy strips the cinematic apparatus of the pleasures of spectatorship; Vernet's flicker, the pulsing of light and dark that brings the image to life, has been run through the machine.

The photocopy is central to much of Cha's work: Alison Fraser's recent study of Cha and xerography notes her "seven artist's books from photocopies or by photocopying," connecting this work to the "material significance of copies" in "deeply interrelated institutions, particularly as it is fixed to various state apparatuses."[13] Through Fraser's particular focus on the Xerox machine, she

---

[8] Roland Barthes, "Upon Leaving the Movie Theater," in *Apparatus*, 1–4, at 1.   [9] Ibid., 3.

[10] Ibid., 3, 4.   [11] Ibid., 4.

[12] Thy Phu, "Decapitated Forms: Theresa Hak Kyung Cha's Visual Text and the Politics of Visibility," *Mosaic* 38.1 (2005): 17–36, at 28.

[13] Alison Fraser, "Diasporic Object Lessons: Material Identity and the Korean Diaspora in the Work of Theresa Hak Kyung Cha," *Women's Studies Quarterly* 47.1&2 (2019): 31–47, at 32, 34.

spells out the link between the cinematic apparatus and the ideological state apparatus. "In the two-tonal medium of xerography," Fraser writes, "Cha literally confronts black-and-white notions about Korean identity, creating sites of self-possession from which she contends with exile, history, and materiality."[14] Cha's particular practice of copying copies in her art disintegrates the photograph into blacks and whites, blurring the diegesis to expose the broader functioning of apparatuses of power.

In this work of exposure, Fraser reads a means of "subverting the hegemonic power structure," and she cites Johanna Drucker's "possibility of the 'democratic multiple'" to argue for xerography as "an opportunity for poetic expression and political commentary."[15] The photocopy instigates aesthetic and political subversions, all the while registering loss and degradation. Fraser's analysis is especially astute in reading the photocopy as marked by temporal and spatial distance; when Cha xeroxes a family photograph over and over again, she records her increasing separation from her family members. Fraser underscores the dynamism of this work, which requires a series – we need to see the change from still to still. This is a dynamism fashioned out of degradation: the moving image xeroxed into a threadbare apparatus in which image, artist, and spectator record the ravages of time and distance.

Cha's copies reveal an expansive understanding of the apparatus, from the flash of the cinematic apparatus to the repressive apparatus of the state. The cinematic black and white, too, produces acts of identification that can collapse subjects at the mercy of repressive apparatuses. Joseph Jeon's reading of Cha's "language art" – Jeon's apt and capacious term for the breadth of Cha's work – turns to Frantz Fanon's *Black Skin White Masks* to consider Cha's engagement with racial form. Jeon features a telling passage in Fanon that recasts Barthes's cinematic attachment:

> The Negro is a toy in the white man's hands; so, in order to shatter the hellish cycle, he explodes. I cannot go to a film without seeing myself. I wait for me. In the interval, just before the film starts, I wait for me. The people in the theater are watching me, examining me, waiting for me. A Negro groom is going to appear. My heart makes my head swim.[16]

Fanon's hell is the abject other to Barthes's narcissism: the Black body is the toy both on the screen and in the theater. Against Barthes's doubled pleasure, Fanon's anticipation entails a fracturing that promises to shatter the self. This is a hell of identification, in which the operations of the cinematic apparatus shackle the body in the theater to the body on screen.

---

[14] Ibid., 32.   [15] Ibid., 34, 34, 42.

[16] Frantz Fanon, *Black Skin White Masks* (New York: Grove Press, 1967), 140.

"The Negro groom is going to appear": the Black spectator is cast onto the screen, the cynosure of all eyes including his own. In this double abjection, Vernet's black-and-white "convergence" is a prison of identification. Jeon reads against whiteness as blankness in Cha's work, and he exposes the filmic apparatus as "part of the larger cultural apparatus that sanctions and perpetuates racist objectification."[17] *Dictée* indicates this larger cultural apparatus within scenes of identification played out in occupying regimes; its speaker inhabits suffering others in disintegrating black and white.

Juliana Spahr's 1996 description of *Dictée* as "part autobiography, part biography, part personal diary, part ethnography, part autoethnography, part translation" spells out its multiple aspects of life writing.[18] Between autobiography and autoethnography we can see, in generic terms, the distance marked out by Barthes and Fanon: Cha's art resides in the span between Barthes's admiring spectatorship and Fanon's swimming head. She sees herself, she waits for herself – and she reveals the black and white of a cinematic apparatus bound to the black-and-white operations of political occupation. *Dictée* is defined by its exquisite awareness of self and others, in which Cha waits, too, for a host of inhabiting others. Historical figures and colonial documents pervade the text, but history is what hurts on an autobiographical plane in *Dictée*. Cha has tasked herself with the labor of tracing out the apparatus of cultural and political identification, all the while featuring her own movements: to read *Dictée* is to follow the career of Cha's identifications – and Cha herself, caught in the play between light and dark.

Alter Ego

Seeded through the cinematic meditations of *Apparatus* are a set of unannounced literary excerpts: unmentioned in the table of contents, they appear on black, unnumbered pages. Mayumo Inoue's reading of specters in Cha's work contemplates these little-considered excerpts as a "haunted apparatus" to connect them to *Dictée*'s "secretive images of history."[19] Inoue identifies Cha's intervention in these spectral passages; their darkened pages show us her hand. These excerpts are literary irruptions that break out of the time capsule of *Apparatus*, to plunge us into an apparatus that transposes the nexus of film-author-spectator into a textual realm. This movement across media, conducted through ghostly means, installs a self-reflexive spirit.

---

[17] Joseph Jeon, *Racial Things, Racial Forms: Objecthood in Avant-Garde Asian American Poetry* (Iowa City: University of Iowa Press, 2012), 38.

[18] Juliana Spahr, "Postmodernism, Readers, and Theresa Hak Kyung Cha's *DICTÉE*," *College Literature* 23.3 (1996): 22–43, at 24.

[19] Mayumo Inoue, "Theresa Hak Kyung Cha's 'Phantomnation': Cinematic Specters and Spectral Collectivity in *Dictée* and *Apparatus*" *Criticism* 56.1 (2014): 63–87, at 80.

The last and longest of these excerpts is drawn from "The Jolly Corner," the most autobiographical of Henry James's short stories. With this story, Cha provides a literary rendering of the workings of the apparatus in a scene of self-confrontation. James's story presents his protagonist waiting for himself in terror – but as with all of James, it is his own hand that presides, and in these dark pages, Cha can reveal the author, the first and most mysterious term of the tripartite cinematic apparatus. Baudry's third essay in *Apparatus*, "Author and Analyzable Subject," turns to literature as a model for authorship, a role complicated by "too many intermediaries" in cinema:[20] "The author is identified by the specific manner in which he uses language," Baudry writes, going on to identify an indescribable "something": "an intelligence, a vision of the world, and, better yet, a style."[21] Between James's inimitable style and Cha's, the author takes the stage – and the particular imbrication of James himself within "The Jolly Corner" makes it special exhibit for the manifestation of the author within his text.

"The Jolly Corner" is a ghost story, and Cha has selected its climactic moment: a black-and-white revelation. James's protagonist Spencer Brydon has returned to his childhood home after thirty-three years in Europe; with the death of his remaining relations, he is to take charge of the family holdings. Brydon's bon vivant decades, funded by these properties, kept these concerns an ocean away, but to his surprise he discovers a hidden aptitude for this business. He oversees the architectural conversion of one property and retreats into the second, his childhood home, on "the jolly corner": he has taken to wandering the empty house at night, searching for the self he left behind for his European exile.

The characteristic "densely intangible prose texture" of Henry James, particularly in his late works, materializes Brydon's doppelganger in this story: as Mark Schiebe puts it in a recent reappraisal of the story, "We are always hunting referents" in James's sentences, and the particular extravagance of "The Jolly Corner" "seems to submerge the human agent in a world of parading mental 'objects.'"[22] As Brydon prowls the corridors, we trace back through grammatical thickets; we parse James's antecedents as his fictional alter ego searches out his double. The hunt consumes Brydon, whose return to New York society becomes a mere backdrop for his nightly adventures: "He projected himself all day, in thought, straight over the bristling line of hard unconscious heads and into the other, the real, the waiting life; the life that, as soon as he had heard

---

[20] Jean-Louis Baudry, "Author and Analyzable Subject," in *Apparatus*, 67–83, at 70.

[21] Ibid., 71.

[22] Mark Schiebe, "Stereo Rivalry in James's 'The Jolly Corner,'" *American Literary Realism* 50.1 (2017): 49–62, at 60.

behind him the click of his great house-door, began for him, on the jolly corner."[23] This projection intimates the moving image, which is "the real, the waiting life"; the click of the house-door readily translates into the silent, swinging doors of the cinema.

It is worth pausing over Brydon's entry into the grand house: "the old marble of the hall pavement, large black-and-white squares that he remembered as the admiration of his childhood and that had then made in him, as he now saw, for the growth of an early conception of style" (317). The formative experience of the marble tiles governs, too, the style of this story: Terry Thompson reads "the neutral black-and-white palette that permeates the entire story, rendering it starkly photographic in imagery and atmosphere."[24] Photographs offer a precision into past memories, and the application of the camera eye to Brydon's wanderings conjures up a counterfactual existence.

Brydon delights in the ritual of doing "ever the same thing; he put his stick noiselessly away in a corner – feeling the place once more in the likeness of some great glass bowl, all precious concave crystal, set delicately humming by the play of a moist finger round its edge" (317). This crystal world of parading things is governed by the hand that plays along the bowl's edge: a figuration of Brydon's feeling for the space that showcases the hand of the narration, of James's authorship. From Brydon's noiseless action to the hum of the glass bowl, we can trace the interdependent operations of the story's apparatus.

What results is a moving image: "His *alter ego* 'walked'" (318). With this certainty, Brydon determines to "'cultivate' his whole perception" – which in turn produces "the recognition – absolutely unmistakeable" of "his being definitely followed" (320). In cultivating his perceptions, Brydon has fashioned his own double – and made himself into a fellow, haunting familiar. This is a circling pursuit, each stalking the other through the space of the empty house. Through his studied self-cultivation, he has entered the world of his other self – to become its hunted object. Through Spencer Brydon, James demonstrates how to materialize this other life.

Cha's excerpt from "The Jolly Corner" features Brydon's climactic encounter with his double. Their reunion – "this time at last they *were*, the two, the opposed projections of him, in presence" (324) – occurs after a full and trembling circuit of the house. The passage in *Apparatus* begins at the moment when Brydon suddenly determines to "sacrifice" the house: "They might come in now, the builders, the destroyers – they might come as soon as they would"

---

[23] Henry James, "The Jolly Corner," *Ghost Stories of Henry James* (Wordsworth Editions, 2001), 317. Subsequent page numbers in parentheses.

[24] Terry Thompson, "That 'Beautiful Art': Black-and-White Photography in Henry James's 'The Jolly Corner,'" *Interdisciplinary Literary Studies* 18.3 (2016): 395–412, at 403.

(328). His prolonged tour of its grand spaces has produced an increasing terror; having lost his mastery of the space, Brydon renounces it.

At dawn, in the black-and-white entry hall, Brydon finally encounters his other self: "The penumbra, dense and dark, was the virtual screen of a figure which stood in it as still as some image erect in a niche or as some black-vizored sentinel guarding a treasure" (329). This screen bristles with objects: the figure, the treasure – and Brydon himself, who is the shadow-casting object that casts this "dense and dark" penumbra. Both are objects in this empty, crystal space, and against Brydon's newfound desire to shatter this glass bowl, his other stands guard as its proper sentinel. James writes out the emergence of this other: "It gloomed, it loomed, it was something, it was somebody, the prodigy of a personal presence" (329). The simple, repetitive, and additive logic of this sentence offers a set of doubled "its" that can be parsed into the matching figures (one glooms, the other looms) to culminate in this "prodigy," or this model in which each is the prodigy of the other.

Here is James's portrait of Brydon's alter ego:

> his planted stillness, his vivid truth, his grizzled bent head and white masking hands, his queer actuality of evening-dress, of dangling double eyeglass, of gleaming silk lappet and white linen, of pearl button and gold watchguard and polished shoe. No portrait by a great modern master could have presented him with more intensity, thrust him out of his frame with more art, as if there had been "treatment," of the consummate sort, in his every shade and salience. (329)

Thompson underscores that this "modern master" is "pointedly described not as a painter" to suggest that James had photographic portraits in mind – perhaps Edward Steichen's photograph of John Pierpont Morgan, likely seen during James's visit to his London estate – to argue that Brydon encounters "a crisp, formally posed, and near photographic 'portrait' of himself as a Gilded Age robber baron."[25] The portrait captures a brutality that fells Brydon: one of the "splendid covering hands" "had lost two fingers, which were reduced to stumps" (329), which Brydon's double lowers to reveal an "unknown, inconceivable, awful" face (330).

As this face advances on Brydon, the photographic portrait becomes cinematic: "It came upon him nearer now, quite as one of those expanding fantastic images projected by the magic lantern of childhood" (330). Brydon's style was fashioned out of the black-and-white tiles of the hall; his terror returns him to a childhood projection. In his encounter with the "vivid truth" of the person he would have been had he heeded his father's wishes and remained in New York, James presents the exile's fantasy, governed by the black-and-white precision of the photograph, both as a glorious still and its animation, into a moving image of terror.

---

[25] Ibid., 409, 408.

The black and white of "The Jolly Corner" details, with photographic precision, how Spencer Brydon cultivates himself to become a ghost. The formative tiles of his childhood beckon him into a glass house to encounter the life he left behind. James's autobiographical tale presents a test of the conjuring powers of the exile, who fashions his alter ego within a photographic apparatus through which the spectator can encounter his own image. But this image becomes a source of terror when it advances onto its maker: once projected into life, the alter ego acquires a rogue agency.

Cha's excerpt in *Apparatus* concludes with Brydon's collapse before his other self's "rage of personality." The life unleashed in black and white: this generative and perilous possibility runs through *Dictée*. While the particular longing of the exile brings a monstrous other to life in "The Jolly Corner," *Dictée*'s speaker bodies forth others, at the risk of her own integrity. James's extraordinarily cultivated style ultimately imperils his protagonist; Cha's style, no less cultivated, exhibits the threat of disintegration at the level of her language. Cha's xerographic black and white strips away the luster of James's photographic apparatus to materialize an author whose hand, while setting the crystal humming, also bears the mutilations of the alter ego.

Tragedy

The paradigmatic space of the movie theater lies at the heart of *Dictée*. Anne Anlin Cheng's critical elaboration that "*Dictée* is not interested in identities, it is profoundly interested in the processes of *identification*" in her landmark 2000 study *The Melancholy of Race* comes into detailed focus in the darkened halls of *Dictée*.[26] Mayumi Takada, in her illuminating 2006 reading "Annihilating Possibilities: Witnessing and Testimony through Cinematic Love in Theresa Hak Kyung Cha's *Dictée*," examines the processes of identification featured in *Apparatus* as a way of comprehending *Dictée*'s operations. Returning to Cha's preface to the anthology, Takada underscores Cha's "bid to make transparent the actual act of identification to suggest that the viewer is not a passive, helpless victim of the filmic lure, but a willing participant." Takada spells out the complexity of this participation: "Instead of revealing itself seducing the audience, film encourages the viewer to seamlessly make multiple, contradictory identifications with the camera's gaze, as well as with the characters on the screen."[27]

---

[26] Anne Anlin Cheng, *The Melancholy of Race: Psychoanalysis, Assimilation, and Hidden Grief* (New York: Oxford University Press, 2000), 141.

[27] Mayumi Takada, "Annihilating Possibilities: Witnessing and Testimony through Cinematic Love in Theresa Hak Kyung Cha's *Dictée*," *Literature Interpretation Theory* 17 (2006): 23–48, at 36, 38.

The "filmic lure" instigates reflexive interrogations of these processes of identification in *Dictée*, through the magnified precision of the camera eye.

Dictée enters the movie theater in "Melpomene / Tragedy," which opens with the spectator: "She could be seen sitting in the first few rows."[28] The light dims in the theater, "gently, slowly until dark," and then she "pulls her coat just below her chin enveloped in one mass" – to face a total onslaught:

> The submission is complete. Relinquishes even the vision to immobility. Abandons all protests to that which will appear to the sight. About to appear. Forecast. Break. Break, by all means. The illusion that the act of viewing is to make alteration of the visible. The expulsion is immediate. Not one second is lost to the replication of the totality. Total severance of the seen. Incision. (79)

This totality threatens the open theorizing of the apparatus, whose conceptualization Cha suggests in "the act of viewing is to make alteration of the visible" – yet in this theater, this is mere "illusion," and "even the vision" is immobile.

At the heart of "Melpomene / Tragedy" is a letter written to her mother during Cha's return to Korea, eighteen years after the family's migration to the United States. The letter details the totalizing replication of the movie theater: "Nothing has changed, we are at a standstill" (80). Cha captures the tragedy of Korea in its reification, perpetually locked into "Civil War. Cold War. Stalemate" (81). She recalls her mother's past hope, "That one day your country would be your own" (80), and then spells out the devastation of "perpetual exile": "We fight the same war. We are inside the same struggle seeking the same destination" (81). This first-person plural, whose urgency governs this letter, is encased in an "act of viewing" that locks Cha's "I" within the "same crowd": "I feel the tightening of the crowd body" (81). This narrowing, constricting collective entails complete submission: an entirely coercive apparatus.

Within this fixity, however, the second person of the letter abruptly shifts focus, from Cha's mother, the addressee of the letter, to a convoy of soldiers in camouflage Cha encounters on the street: "You soldiers appear in green": "You are your post you are your vow in nomine patris you work your post you are your nation defending your country from subversive infiltration from your own countrymen" (86). Something happens with these synecdochic identifications: the very rigidity of this "you" breaks it open in a contradiction of a total identification with the state that detaches you "from your own countrymen." The fracture between state and nation, "your country" and "your countrymen": this is the nightmare of civil war, defined by the simultaneous making and unmaking of the distinction between friend and enemy, self and other.

---

[28] *Dictée* (Berkeley, CA: Third Woman Press, 1995), 79. Subsequent page numbers in parentheses.

So the soldiers – "you cannot be seen behind the guns" – morph into their target:

> You are hidden you see only the prey they do not see you they cannot. You
> who are hidden you who move in the crowds as you would in the trees you
> who move inside them you close your eyes to the piercing the breaking the
> flooding pools bath their shadow memory as they fade from you your own
> blood your own flesh as tides ebb, through you through and through. (86)

These lines end the prose of the section to shift into a lyric register, and they
bewilder the distinction between the camouflaged soldiers ("You are hidden")
and their prey among their countrymen ("You who are hidden"). The movement of this other "you," eyes closed "to the piercing the breaking," experiences the intimacy of this most vicious of wars, against "your own blood your
own flesh."

Civil war threatens the identity of "you" because it operates "through you
through and through." The perpetual danger of reversal lies at the heart of
fratricidal war: you against your mirror image. That this reversal is also an
opening permits the movement from Melpomene to Erato, tragedy to love: the
section ends in a lyric mode that recasts the doubled "you" of the soldiers and
their prey into the predominating pronouns of *Dictée*: "SHE opposes Her. /
SHE against her. / More than that" (87). This "more" beyond the conflict is
a call to "arrest the screen" (88), and then, "Arrest the machine that purports to
employ democracy but rather causes the successive refraction of her none
other than her own" (89). This "successive refraction" names the apparatus of
the state "that purports to employ democracy," a perpetuation notably cast in
the language of bending light. "Melpomene / Tragedy" closes with "she" and
"her" in unison:

> Suffice Melpomene, to exorcize from this mouth the name the words the
> memory of severance through this act by this very act to utter one, *Her* once,
> Her to utter at once. *She* without the separate act of uttering. (89)

This exorcism through the name of Melpomene sutures together these pronouns, object and subject. "Melpomene / Tragedy" arrests the apparatus of the
state to reconsider the possibilities of a divided self.

In thus laying bare ideological apparatuses through a process of identification
inseparable from its mode of capture, the operations of *Dictée* are necessarily
social acts. Cha's aesthetic acts are unfree, not only because she answers to
political structures, but because the processes of identification she unveils are
social, collective. Cheng's reading of *Dictée* explains that Cha, "defined by the
traumatic history of her 'heritage,'" is at once "dispossessed by that inheritance
with equal vehemence" because "no one can be at the center"; indeed, Cheng

reveals the core difficulty of *Dictée* in the way it "implicates, in fact, our positions as private, historical, or literary witnesses of submerged histories."[29]

Such social contours instigate Hyo Kim's 2013 reading of *Dictée*, which demonstrates how "Cha's text theorizes the self as constitutively entangled in and by the social." Considering the collective orientation of the text, Kim argues that "*Dictée*'s embodied vision of writing radically undermines the traditional author function," to conclude: "*Dictée* – no matter how personal it may seem – is entangled in a disjointed, overdetermined collective narrative."[30] *Dictée* comprehends the worlds – political and ghostly – that ensnare aesthetic operations, and it details the impossibility of an inviolable self in underworlds and dream worlds.

Cinematic Love

Mayumi Takada critiques a (continuing) scholarly tendency to focus on *Dictée*'s first half, significantly devoted to imperial atrocity, over the "ignored latter sections" that "most resemble Cha's work as a whole." Takada's reading zeroes in on "the Erato section which appears literally at the center of the work and marks an obvious shift from the personal and ethnic to the impersonal and ethnically unmarked." The center point of Erato balances the "coercive violence" detailed in the first half with a "utopian possibility of witnessing and testimony": Takada maps out a cinematic mode of identification through witness, which provides an opening, a measure of love in the face of history and tragedy.[31] My return to this heart of *Dictée* tracks the precision of its captivating mode, its cinematic operations in black and white.

From the union of she and her at the close of "Melpomene / Tragedy," Cha returns to the movie theater in "Erato / Love Poetry," which is, as Trinh T. Minh-ha puts it, "significantly written as a film script."[32] The section features two running threads of narration intercut across its recto and verso pages, and through its montage, "Erato / Love Poetry" offers a radical reconsideration of the total submission in the theater presented in "Melpomene / Tragedy." The section opens with the entry into the theater – "She is entering now" – rendered in painstaking detail:

---

[29] Cheng, *Melancholy of Race*, 149, 150.

[30] Hyo Kim, "Embodying the In-Between: Theresa Hak Kyung Cha's Dictée," *Mosaic* 46.4 (2013) : 127–143, at 136. José Felipe Alvergue's "Poetic Seeing / Beyond Telling: The 'Call' in Theresa Hak Kyung Cha's *Dictée*," *College Literature* 43.2 (2016): 427–456, suggests the concept of a crowd without the category of the social.

[31] Takada, "Annihilating Possibilities," 24, 25, 46.

[32] Trinh T. Minh-ha, "White Spring," in *The Dream of the Audience: Theresa Hak Kyung Cha (1951–1982)*, edited by Constance M. Lewallen (Berkeley: University of California Press, 2001), 33–49, at 48.

> She hands her ticket to the usher and climbs three steps, into the room. The
> whiteness of the screen takes her back wards almost half a step. Then she
> proceeds again to the front. Near front. Close to the screen. She takes the
> fourth seat from the left. The utmost center of the room. She sees on her left
> the other woman, the same woman in her place as the day before. (94)

The "other woman" recalls the huddled figure in the theater of Melpomene, but
the formal montage of these pages directs our eye across to the next line,
positioned on the recto page:

> Whiteness of the screen. Takes her backwards. (94)

This line, repeated and fractured across the facing page, isolates the agency of
the screen's whiteness. This screen registers the black and white of the apparatus, and in the following passage, returning to the verso page, the film begins:

> She enters the screen from the left, before the titles fading in and fading out.
> The white subtitles on the black background continue across the bottom of the
> screen. The titles and names in black appear from the upper right hand corner,
> each letter moving downwards on to the whiteness of the screen. She is drawn
> to the white, then the black. In the whiteness the shadows move across, dark
> shapes and dark light. (94)

This cinematic reprise of the opening "She is entering now" situates this "she"
amid the black and white of the titles, to suture the figure in the audience to the
figure on the screen: both are "drawn to the white, then the black" – a line then
picked up on the recto page.

   This black and white is a figuration of the cinematic apparatus, and the
doubled entry into the theater counters Barthes's "Upon Leaving the Movie
Theater," cutting away from narcissistic identification to the mirrored entry of
"she" on the screen who instead resonates with Fanon's anticipatory "I wait for
myself." Fanon's dread does not feature in Cha's scenario, but the montage she
fashions interrogates the pleasure of identification. For Barthes, the filmic
image is a "lure" that "ensnares me, captures me" (3) so thoroughly that he
calls upon a second, "perverse body" to fashion "a 'relationship' with the
'situation'" (4). By contrast, Cha activates a relationship between film and
spectator that lays bare the work of the apparatus: projected onto the screen,
we must register the spectator within the terms of black and white.

   The page that follows rewrites the entry into the theater into the technical
specifications of the cinematic apparatus: "Close Up shot of her feet from the
back on the three steps leading into the theatre, camera following her from the
back" (96). Cha's mirroring of film to spectator reveals the hand of "the author
of the film," and this reprise notes "the other woman" in the theater as well:

The theatre is empty, she is turning right into the aisle and moving forward. She selects a row near the front, fourth seat from the left and sits. Medium Close Up, directly from behind her head. She turns her head to the left, on her profile. Camera pans left and remains still at the profile of another woman seated. Camera pans back to the right, she turns her head to the front. The screen fades to white. (96)

The intercut facing-page thread, thus far engaged in punctuating the black and white of the movement into the theater – "The shadows moving across the whiteness, dark shapes and dark light" (95) – now shifts to speech: "Mouth moving. Incessant. Precise. Forms the words heard. Moves from the mouth to the ear" (97). From the panning movement of the camera between the two spectators to these mouth formations, Cha's montage intimates a conversation between them: they communicate through the mouth on the screen.

This is a mode of communication that operates across the surface of the screen, and I see this mouth moving between these two women: "She forms the words with her mouth as the other utter across from her" (99). We discover that the mouth says, "On verra," and then, "She hears, we will see" – which launches a series of appeals:

We would wait. Wait to see, We would have to wait to see, Wait and see. If. For a second time. For another time. For the other overlapping time. Too fast. Slow your pace. Please. Slower, much slower. For me to follow. Doucement. Lentement. Softly and slowly. For a second time. For another time. Two times. Together. (99)

This "we" intimates the two women in the theater – the "she" of Melpomene and that of Erato – appealing to the cinematic apparatus: "Slow your pace," "softly and slowly." They call for a moderation in pace and tone that Fanon could not. As they wait and see together, they effect an intercutting between times; as spectators, they harness a cinematic capacity to address the "author of the film."[33]

Cha then cuts in with what we will see:

One expects her to be beautiful. The title which carries her name is not one that would make her anonymous or plain. "The portrait of . . . " (98)

This is our movie: the portrait of a beautiful name. This narrative thread runs along the verso pages, and in Cha's painstaking direction I see the interplay of the author, between film and spectator. After this gesture toward the film's title, Cha shows us how the movie works on our expectations:

---

[33] It is worth noting too this work of translation in which a phrase that is commonplace in French acquires a temporal opening in the carry over to English: the future tense of "on verra" becomes an opportunity for extending duration as it morphs into "wait and see."

> One seems to be able to see her. One imagines her, already. Already before
> the title. She is not seen right away. Her image, yet anonymous suspends in
> one's mind. With the music on the sound track you are prepared for her
> entrance. More and more. You are shown the house in which she lives, from
> the outside. (98)

She is an image in our minds that precedes the film's title, music, and establish-
ing shots. In leading with the pre- or extra-cinematic dimensions of this
portrait – she already "suspends in the mind" – Cha is recording the ability of
the spectator to condition what she sees. This is not, however, to fall sway to the
"illusion that the act of viewing is to make alteration of the visible," already
shattered in the theater of "Melpomene"; instead, we comprehend the interplay
between our imagination and the preparatory cues of the film.

   From this approach, Cha goes on to align the movement of the spectator to the film:

> Then you, as a viewer and guest, enter the house. It is you who are entering to
> see her. Her portrait is seen through her things, that are hers. The arrangement
> of her house is spare, delicate, subtly accentuating, rather, the space, not the
> objects that fill the space. Her movements are already punctuated by the
> movement of the camera, her pace, her time, her rhythm. You move from
> the same distance as the visitor, with the same awe, same reticence, same
> anticipation. (98, 100)

Our entry into the house is also an entry into the film's diegesis: as "viewer and
guest," we occupy a place in the story, in which we discover that the portrait we
were expecting "is seen through her things, that are hers." The passive con-
struction of the way in which she is seen presents a situational seeing, and it
entails another sense of the "she" and "her": the possessive. Her claim expands
from her things, to their arrangement, and then to the movements of the camera,
revealing how much she possesses: "her pace, her time, her rhythm." In thus
binding the spectator to the film, Cha indicates an identity across the three terms
of the apparatus, with the author in the center.

   The camera moves through her house:

> Stationary on the light never still on her bath water, then slowly moving from
> room to room, through the same lean and open spaces. Her dress hangs on
> a door, the cloth is of a light background, revealing the surface with
> a landscape stained with the slightest of hues. (100)

We see a world within this interior: the stationary camera captures "light never
still" in the bath and the hanging dress invokes an entire landscape. The
attributes of her space – spare, delicate, subtle, lean, and open – are her portrait,
as we discover by the end of this passage:

> Her portrait is not represented in a still photograph, nor in a painting. All
> along, you see her without actually seeing, actually having seen her. You do
> not see her yet. For the moment, you see only her traces. (100)

Her portrait is not a photograph or a painting because, of course, it is a film: it is
a moving picture. Her portrait is her movement: it is "her" in the possessive and
not the accusative grammatical sense. Ultimately, this pace, time, and rhythm
are the province of the author, and so this is how I complete the title of the film:
The Portrait of Theresa Hak Kyung Cha.

This self-portrait recalls Spencer Brydon's nightly prowls through his childhood home, when he seeks out the life he would have had. The long night that
culminates in his face-to-face encounter with his double exhaustively details
Brydon's tour of the house: this ghost is a product of his movement through the
vast spaces of the house, and he appears when threatened with dispossession. In
Brydon's terror as he discovers proof of his double – a shut door has been
reopened – he renounces the house: "He tried to think of something noble, as
that his property was really grand, a splendid possession; but his nobleness took
the form too of the clear delight with which he was finally to sacrifice it" (327–
328). The sacrifice of this possession finally conjures the appearance of his
double, who steps out of the shadows to do battle.

It is worth recalling that Brydon's doppelganger is a concatenation of things:
"his queer actuality of evening-dress, of dangling double eyeglass, of gleaming
silk lappet and white linen, of pearl button and gold watchguard and polished
shoe" (329). This "actuality," composed of dress and upper-class accoutrements,
is finely detailed and frozen, but at the revelation of his face – "The face, *that* face,
Spencer Brydon's?" (330) – he collapses in horror: the face cannot belong to him.
Unlike the still photograph of his dress, the face is a moving, advancing image.
While James unveils a photographic portrait, Cha's moving portrait eludes
capture: hers is not a representation but a set of possessions. And against
James's "actuality of evening-dress," its "gleaming silk lappet and white linen,"
the dress in Cha's film reveals a background, a landscape: her things are not
assembled into a portrait; instead, they open out to farther spaces. Cha's stills
present movement, and they show us the author, too, roving in pursuit.

Saint Thérèse

The intercut threads of "Erato / Love Poetry" are "presented as simultaneously
discrete and interrelated," as Takada explains: one "reflects the fantasy enactment
of the reader's relation to Cha's text"; the other presents Saint Thérèse of Lisieux.[34]
These halves present two different marriages – sacred and profane – in a cinematic

---

[34] Takada, "Annihilating Possibilities," 32.

montage that threads divine ecstasy into the disappointments of a conventional union. This divine order cuts into the measured movement of the camera that reveals the traces of a portrait in a brash announcement:

> Letter of Invitation to the Wedding of Sister Thérèse of the Child Jesus and the Holy Face.
>
> God Almighty, Creator of Heaven and Earth, Sovereign Ruler of the Universe, the Most Glorious Virgin May, Queen of the Heavenly Court, announce to you the Spiritual Espousal of Their August Son, Jesus, King of kings, and Lord of lords, with little Thérèse Martin, now Princess and Lady of His Kingdoms of the Holy Childhood and the Passion, assigned to her in dowry by her Divine Spouse, from which kingdoms she holds her titles of nobility – of the Child Jesus and the Holy Face.
>
> Monsieur Louis Martin, Proprietor and Master of the Domains of Suffering and Humiliation and Mme Martin, Princess and Lady of Honor of the Heavenly Court, wish to have you take part in the Marriage of their Daughter, Thérèse, with Jesus, the Word of God, the Second Person of the Adorable Trinity, who through the operation of the Holy Spirit was made Man and Son of Mary, Queen of Heaven.
>
> Being unable to invite you to the Nuptial Blessing which was given on Mount Carmel, September 8, 1890 (the heavenly court alone was admitted), you are nevertheless asked to be present at the Return from the Wedding which will take place Tomorrow, the Day of Eternity, on which day Jesus, Son of God, will come on the Clouds of Heaven in the splendor of His Majesty, to judge the Living and the Dead.
>
> The hour being as yet uncertain, you are invited to hold yourself in readiness and watch. (101, 103)

This is astounding excess – a divine union rendered in the wild pomp of a bourgeois wedding announcement. The parents of the bridegroom and the bride are presented with near-comic lavishness, but the strangest aspect of this invitation is its inutility: "Being unable to invite you to the nuptial blessing," you are called instead to Judgment Day, "Tomorrow." This is an invitation to the end-times.

This invitation was composed by "little Thérèse Martin" – who would advance to sainthood in record time – and it is featured in the remarkable autobiography of Saint Thérèse of Lisieux. Cha notes this source in the closing pages of *Dictée*, and I want to dwell on the appearance of Cha's namesake in the center of her masterwork. With Saint Thérèse, we encounter a different order of self-presentation: near the end of her short life – she died of tuberculosis at age twenty-four – Thérèse, then a Carmelite nun in Lisieux, composed a series of letters to her sisters at their behest. Her sister Céline recalled, "She wrote simply through obedience . . . Her manuscript was really a 'family souvenir,' destined exclusively for her sisters" – but upon completing it, Thérèse expressed a grand ambition for this work, telling an older sister and fellow Carmelite at Lisieux: "After my death, you must speak to no one about my manuscript before it is published; you must speak only to Mother Prioress about it. If you act otherwise, the devil will lay more than one trap to hinder God's work, a very important work!"[35] Céline heeded Thérèse's urgent exhortation, and published *Story of a Soul* a year later, in 1898.

Thérèse Martin was the youngest of five sisters who all became nuns. *Story of a Soul* records her passionate longing to become a Carmelite, following her beloved elder sisters. Father Bernard Bro spells out the curiosity of Saint Thérèse: "How are we to understand Thérèse of Lisieux?" he asks. "Of what possible interest is a provincial petite-bourgeoise who enters the cloister? A spirituality inclined to the cult of suffering?" Bro goes on to provide an answer: "Thérèse herself would say: Thérèse is of little importance . . . But what is at stake is one of the most certain and simplest evangelical shortcuts ever proposed."[36] *Story of a Soul* details Thérèse's model of direct connection between the self and the divine, a revelatory shortcut composed of little acts. Describing her "resolution to give myself up more than ever to a *serious* and *mortified* life" (143, original italics) in the months before her entry into Carmel, Thérèse makes a key specification: "When I say mortified, this is not to give the impression that I performed acts of penance" (143). Her acts are smaller:

> My mortifications consisted in breaking my will, always so ready to impose itself on others, in holding back a reply, in rendering little services without any recognition, in not leaning my back against a support when seated, etc., etc. It was through the practice of these sweet *nothings* that I prepared myself to become the fiancée of Jesus. (143–44, original italics)

And so we read in *Story of a Soul* that Thérèse joyfully assists a cantankerous nun and welcomes the splash of dirty water during laundry duty. Thérèse's descriptions of these "nothings" have a phenomenological character: notably detached from larger acts of penance, they detail little aversions.

Mary Frohlich's introduction to Saint Thérèse's plays and poetry situates her family among the French Catholic bourgeoisie of the period, who "lived a largely inward-facing life." Frohlich explains that "many Catholics still configured their personal lives in terms of a black-and-white division between a holy, Church-centered life and the utter moral corruption they perceived in the mainstream culture." "Those who were most caught up in this spirituality,"

---

[35] Saint Thérèse de Lisieux, *Story of a Soul: The Autobiography of St. Thérèse of Lisieux* (Washington, DC: Institute of Carmelite Studies, 2017), xv, xix. Subsequent page numbers in parentheses.

[36] Father Bernard Bro, *Saint Thérèse of Lisieux: Her Family, Her God, Her Message* (San Francisco: Ignatius Press, 2003), 10, 11 (original ellipsis).

Frohlich writes, "often suffered from the affliction of scruples – the all-consuming anxiety that one might be doing something wrong, or in the wrong way, or not doing enough, and that this has radically alienated one from God."[37] Thérèse's strictures regarding every little thing operate in this black-and-white affliction, which pegged every action to devotion. *Story of a Soul* records the apotheosis of such bourgeois scruples, which cut against Thérèse's nature. "Ah! what peace floods the soul when she rises above natural feelings," Thérèse writes as she recalls her novitiate period (226). She concludes this reflection with an echoing cry: "Ah! how contrary are the teachings of Jesus to the feelings of nature!" (229). From "sweet nothings" to this crowning of the unnatural: *Story of a Soul* is a tale of unnatural desires.

In a compelling comparison of Thérèse of Lisieux with her monumental predecessor, Teresa of Avila, Vita Sackville-West describes Saint Thérèse's Little Way: "Never to fail in the smallest particular" in order "to train the character by incessant practice until the eclipsing of self became second nature." In this punishing vigilance, Sackville-West notes, "every privation became a privilege, every loss a gain. The normal attitude to existence is indeed reversed." This "shortcut" replaces miraculous acts with mundane tortures – Sackville-West muses over the contrast to the grand ferocity of Teresa of Avila, citing Pius X's description of Thérèse as "an exquisitely delicate miniature of perfect saintliness." While, as Sackville-West writes, "Teresa of Avila had been flung about by the Devil," it was Thérèse's little, inward trials that captivated modern Catholics. Saint Thérèse's model of self-abnegation, born from bourgeois striving, domesticates great trials.[38]

The bizarre wedding invitation demonstrates this order of translation. We discover in *Story of a Soul* that Thérèse was inspired by her cousin Jeanne's wedding:

> Jeanne's wedding took place eight days after I received the Veil. It would be impossible, dear Mother, for me to tell you how much I learned from her example concerning the delicate attentions a bride can bestow upon her bridegroom. I listened eagerly to what she was saying so that I would learn all I could since I didn't want to do less for my beloved Jesus than Jeanne did for her Francis; true, he was a perfect creature, but he was still only a *creature*!
>
> I even went so far as to amuse myself to composing a letter of invitation which was comparable to Jeanne's own letter, and this is how it was written. (168, original italics)

---

[37] Mary Frohlich, Introduction to *St. Thérèse of Lisieux: Essential Writings*, edited by Mary Frohlich (Maryknoll, NY: Orbis Books, 2003), 13–31, at 17, 18.

[38] Vita Sackville-West, *The Eagle and the Dove: A Study in Contrasts* (London: Michael Joseph, 1943), 130, 128, 131, 139.

Then the invitation. This transposition from creaturely to divine lays bare the bourgeois standard that governs Thérèse's imagination – and it produces a truly unnatural exercise that far exceeds its girlish instigation. The ceremony has already taken place, and so this invitation is in fact an admonition: "The hour being as yet uncertain, you are invited to hold yourself in readiness and watch." Clothed in the lavishness of a glorious wedding, this invitation is in fact a check on behavior and a call to witness. It is an invitation to self-scrutiny. The blast of this invitation holds no traces of the "delicate attentions a bride can bestow upon her bridegroom"; instead, it leads us to a judging God.

The "Letter of Invitation" requires us to "wait and see." If we recall the "on verra" on the screen as a mode of communication between the spectators in the cinema, the extraordinary intrusion of Saint Thérèse, with its broadening and leveling force, folds *Dictée*'s readers in as well. "We would have to wait and see, Wait and see. If. For a second time. For another time, For the other overlapping time": Saint Thérèse's "Tomorrow" is the ultimate other time. "Erato / Love Poetry" reveals *Dictée*'s apparatus through its interplays, founded on the time art of cinema. In assigning us the role of witness, Saint Thérèse opens a messianic time: her announcement catapults us out of empty time into the time of connection, of history reactivated into immediacy.

The miracle of Saint Thérèse is her conversion of the quotidian: bourgeois emptiness charged with the rigors of divine obeisance. Sackville-West names her "the imitable saint" whose "Little Way was a lane, by-passing the main road of the heroic."[39] She was the saint of shortcuts and bypasses and yet her practices were only deceptively easy. The "Letter of Invitation" exposes the unnaturalness of her practice, and her "Tomorrow" is an annihilating time. The Passion of Saint Thérèse was no less an annihilation: her innumerable little trials led the way to a terrifying joy at suffering. She thrills at the worsening symptoms of the tuberculosis that cut short her life: "I had scarcely laid my head upon the pillow when I felt something like a bubbling stream mounting to my lips. I didn't know what it was, but I thought that perhaps I was going to die and my soul was flooded with joy" (210). The morning light confirms blood: "*It was like a sweet and distant murmur that announced the Bridegroom's arrival*" (211, original italics). But this unnatural delight is accompanied by doubt:

> He permitted my soul to be invaded by the thickest darkness, and that the thought of heaven, up until then so sweet to me, be no longer anything but the cause of struggle and torment. This trial was to last not a few days or a few weeks, it was not to be extinguished until the hour set by God himself and this hour has not yet come. (211–212)

---

[39] Ibid., 132.

Guy Gaucher discusses Saint Thérèse's Passion as an "abyss of darkness that made her contemporary with the atheists of her century."[40] It is difficult not to read this darkness as an indication of the unnaturalness, even grotesquerie, of her joy at suffering.

The shortcut of the Little Way is not a guard against agony. Saint Thérèse's deathbed trial presents a further reversal of black and white in which heaven becomes a torment. In her acute suffering, I register a fuller resonance with Cha herself: "Suffering became my attraction" (79), Saint Thérèse notes in her account of her first communion. Expressing her mature comprehension of this longing, she writes that Jesus "has given me the attraction for a complete exile and He has made me *understand all the sufferings* I would meet with" (218 original italics). Cha's intimate knowledge of the suffering of exile resonates with the saintly conversion of a difficult state into a glorious one, and Saint Thérèse's greatest trial, which threatened to reverse the order of all things, plunges into a deeper agony. If Saint Thérèse makes us all into witnesses, she is also subject to the most harrowing trial – and this leveling isolation forms the heart of *Dictée*.

"Until Then"

From Thérèse's exalted announcement in *Dictée*, we return to the verso thread:

> Until then. The others relay her story. She is married to her husband who is unfaithful to her. No reason is given. No reason is necessary except that he is a man. It is a given. (102)

"Until then" marks out the period of this human story. While Thérèse can narrate her own story, the story of an unfaithful husband is relayed by others. Considering the unfathomable gap between "degraded wife and passionately devoted saint," Eleanor Craig spells out what they share: "both positions take for granted expectations of feminine servitude, sacrifice, and even annihilation."[41] Craig's perceptive reading of the "devotional work" presented in *Dictée* reveals a feminine devotional standard that operates across sacred and profane unions. It is Craig's primary contention that *Dictée* is "a study in practices of devotion" that can be liberatory or violent, and the text is ultimately "engaging in purpose-fully ambiguous devotional work."[42] In the doubled exhibit of devotional work in "Erato / Love Poetry," I identify in Saint Thérèse's divine standard a revelatory apparatus that directs us to witness – "you are invited to hold yourself in readiness

---

[40] Guy Gaucher, *The Passion of Thérèse of Lisieux* (New York: Crossroad, 1998), 56.

[41] Eleanor Craig, "The Ambiguity of Devotion: Complicity and Resistance in Theresa Hak Kyung Cha's *DICTÉE*," *Representations* 153 (2021): 85–104, at 97.

[42] Ibid., 86.

and watch" – and in the gaping distance opened by the saint's "Tomorrow" and this human "Until then," I identify Cha's movements.

"Stands the distance between the husband and wife the distance of heaven and hell": this is how the husband enters the scene, governed by his movements and voice. The passage continues:

> The husband is seen. Entering the house shouting her name, calling her name. You find her for the first time as he enters the room calling her. You only hear him taunting and humiliating her. She kneels beside him, putting on his clothes for him. She takes her place. It is given. It is the night of her father's wake, she is in mourning. Still the apprenticeship of the wife to her husband. (102, 104)

Rendering the husband in a passive voice, Cha reserves the second-person address – our entry into the story – for finding her. Her mourning as a daughter is preempted by her duty as a wife, and Cha's "apprenticeship" resonates with the graduated process of the convent, which seals the novitiate away from her family. Cha's direction pinpoints its focus:

> He leaves the room. She falls to the floor, your eyes move to the garden where water is dripping into the stone well from the bark of a tree. And you need not see her cry. (104)

This aesthetic displacement, which reroutes our gaze to a natural scene, follows a precise, imagistic strategy designed to capture a flash of feeling. The tenets of imagist poetry were fashioned from cinematic theories of montage and a vogue for Far Eastern poetics in the early twentieth century – and they come together here, in Cha's filmic haiku. The haiku is a poem of place and season that conveys a precise feeling out of juxtaposition: it is a situating and detaching art that relies on presentation of place to depict a sensation that can be felt elsewhere, in other times.

So much of this story is a presentation of its environment, from the interior landscape of the house to Cha's direction away from the falling woman, to the garden. The movement of our eyes is necessarily that of the camera: the water "dripping into the stone well from the bark of a tree" requires a close-up. It goes without saying that what we see is Cha's hand, in a highly deliberate exhibit of "the author of the film": she is director and poet here, and in guiding us to what we "need not see," she is fashioning our own feelings. The verso thread of this story extends this finely tuned connection, which transfers movement and feeling from the screen / page to the spectator / reader. Cha carries this story through a set of locations: the lake, whose surface records the passage of a full day from dawn to moonlight; the pines and hills beyond the lake; a room with a piano; the restaurant by the lake where she has ordered a cup of tea. Throughout these scenes, Cha directs us to the presence of the screen and to our position as spectators: all components of relaying her story.

It is worth dwelling on Cha's exposition of her movements:

> She moves slowly. Her movements are made gradual, dull, made to extend from inside her, the woman, her, the wife, her walk weighted full to the ground. Stillness that follows when she closes the door. She cannot disturb the atmosphere. The space where she might sit. When she might. She moves in its pauses. She yields space and in her speech, the same. Hardly speaks. Hardly at all. The slowness of her speech when she does. Her tears her speech. (104)

This is acting direction that requires the star of the film to yield, inside and out. Her walk, extending from a bodily interior lodged within the given role of the wife, is "weighted full to the ground," and her movements "cannot disturb the atmosphere." Heavy movements and slow, bare speech: this is the movement of the wife. All of this yielding, and her tears, already given over to the garden, are continuous with the atmosphere she is powerless to disrupt.

Yet this atmosphere allows us in:

> Upon seeing her you know how it was for her. You know how it might have been. You recline, you lapse, you fall, you see before you what you have seen before. Repeated, without your even knowing it. It is you standing there. It is you waiting outside in the summer day. It is you waiting and knowing to wait. How to. Wait. (106)

Cha's art here is to create the atmosphere for our entry, in not showing "her" but her world. "Erato / Love Poetry" has matched the total submission to the cinema depicted in "Melpomene / Tragedy" with the duty of the wife to produce an order of recognition that conscripts the spectator into these ceding acts. Across this total identification is the waiting that we share, dictated from on high – in the text through the vehicle of Saint Thérèse invitation and, above even this heavenly order, Cha herself, who is directing us on "How to. Wait."

With our entry, identifications proliferate: "It is you walking a few steps before the man who walks behind you," and "Then it becomes you, the man, her companion" (106) as the movie scene shifts to a past interior. Something different happens here: "You look through the window and the music fills and breaks the entire screen from somewhere. Else. From else where" (108). As remembered music breaks the screen, this filmic space has broken into memory. Then, once on the terrain of memory, we discover a completely new order of interaction: "You walk inside the room" (108) and then

> She asks if you want to sing a song and you move next to her on the bench and you sing for her as she plays for you. (110)

Like the music from elsewhere, we have entered the diegesis to sit beside her and even to sing – and she accompanies us.

As we come to occupy the screen, she becomes more elusive and this story thread both expands and scatters, momentarily harking back to the early days of the marriage ("In the beginning it was different" [110]) to settle back on the claims of the husband. The story cuts away: "She forgets. She tries to forget. For the moment. For the duration of these moments" (113). This longing for oblivion effects a pervading whiteness:

> The white mist rising everywhere, constant gathering and dispersing. This is how it fills the screen. (112)

The story has built to this supremely self-referential moment in which the whiteness of the page becomes the mist-filled screen. The screen thus filled is the blank screen: this white is a revelation of the apparatus. Then, in the passage that follows on the recto page, the woman eclipsed by this white shows her hand:

> She opens the cloth again. White. Whitest of beige. In the whiteness, subtle hues outlining phoenix from below phoenix from above facing each other in the weave barely appearing. Disappearing into the whiteness. (113)

The montage matches the white of the cloth to the white of the screen – which in turn matches the woman to "the author of the screen," Cha herself. With this transposition, we can peer into the white mist to discover "subtle hues," the outline of a pattern of birds. The woman "cannot disturb the atmosphere," but in opening the cloth, she lays out the screen. This is the opening afforded in the rigor of Cha's apparatus, in which inside and outside are subject to the same properties and made of the same stuff.

We learn that this cloth was once intended to be sewn into a quilt, but now, as the woman "looks at it once more with a vague uneasiness," she acts:

> It stings her inside. All sudden. Summons. Move. To simply move. Her body. Renounce no more the will inhabiting her. Complete. She changes her dress, shed to the ground, left as it fell.
>
> She moves now. Quickly. You trace her steps just after, as soon as, she leaves the frame. She leaves them empty. You are following her. Inside the mist. Close. She is buried there. You lose her. It occurs to you, her name. Suddenly. Snow. The mist envelops her she appears from it. Far. (114)

The white cloth instigates a summons: "Renounce no more." With the revelation of the screen, she leaves us behind: "she leaves the frame. She leaves them empty." I see this "sting" as the realization of the apparatus: she understands that she can leave the screen. Her name "occurs" to us upon her departure because the empty frame leaves us with the "author of the film," whose name is that of the guiding saint: Theresa.

The final page of the story takes us back outside the movie theater: "It had been snowing. During the while." That the sudden snow on the screen has fallen outside the theater indicates the full dimensions of Cha's apparatus. The closing lines of the "Erato / Love Poetry" spell out what has happened to her:

> In the whiteness
> no distinction her body invariable no dissonance
> synonymous her body all the time de composes
> eclipses to be come yours. (118)

She has become us. The through-and-through identifications and reversals of "Erato / Love Poetry" effect a remarkable but also annihilating liberation: she has escaped by eclipsing herself. This is a freedom akin to Saint Thérèse's "Tomorrow," in both cases a disintegrating apotheosis. *Dictée* is a study of the lost integrity of the self, and the innovation of Cha's cinematic and self-referential form details how we enter her work, which in turn pervades who we are.

"I Choose All!"

Saint Thérèse's ringing convictions punctuate "Erato / Love Poetry." Cut into the cinematic tale, she serves as both guide and scourge. The second of the five passages Cha has excerpted from *Story of a Soul* is drawn from Thérèse's pilgrimage to Rome, where she secured an audience with the pope to petition for entry into the Carmelite convent at Lisieux despite her youth. Cha has selected Thérèse's meditation on the treatment of women:

> I still cannot understand why women are so easily excommunicated in Italy, for every minute someone was saying, "Don't enter here! Don't enter there, you will be excommunicated!" Ah poor women, how they are misunderstood! And yet they love God in much larger numbers than men do and during the Passion of Our Lord, women had more courage than the apostles since they braved the insults of the soldiers and dared to dry the adorable Face of Jesus. He allows misunderstanding to be their lot on earth since He chose it for Himself. In heaven, He will show that His thoughts are not men's thoughts, for then the last will be first. (105)

She can only make sense of this injustice in the unnatural black and white of her devotion, in which privation converts to privilege; these "poor women" have only to wait until "the last will be the first." Despite this consolation, the passage does not conceal her outrage, and what follows Cha's excerpted passage in *Story of a Soul* is revealing: "More than once during the trip I hadn't the patience to await heaven to be first" (140), she writes, going on to detail an episode in which she disobeyed "Don't enter here!" signals at a Carmelite monastery in Italy.

Thérèse herself can't wait until tomorrow, and *Story of a Soul* is shot through with her overweening desires. She recounts a story from her childhood, when an elder sister offers a basket of toys she has outgrown to Thérèse and Céline: "Céline stretched out her hand and took a little ball of wool that pleased her. After a moment's reflection, I stretched out mine saying: 'I choose all!' and I took the basket without further ceremony" (27). This outsize claim echoes in another excerpt Cha features in "Erato / Love Poetry":

> Martyrdom was the dream of my youth and this dream has grown with me within Carmel's cloisters. But here again, I feel that my dream is a folly, for I cannot confine myself to desiring one kind of martyrdom. To satisfy me I need all. Like You, my Adorable Spouse, I would be scourged and crucified. I would die flayed like St. Bartholomew. I would be plunged into boiling oil like St. John; I would undergo all the torture inflicted upon the martyrs. With St. Agnes and St. Cecilia, I would present my neck to the sword, and like Joan of Arc, my dear sister, I would whisper at the stake Your Name, O JESUS. (117, original emphasis)

The child who seized the toy basket continues to grasp at all: the dream of her youth has only grown. It is worth noting that for Thérèse, the folly is not the dream but its confinement. *Story of a Soul* is a record of wild, ungovernable desires confined within the black and white of bourgeois Catholicism. Even the excesses of her nuptial announcement cannot accommodate this desire to be "Like You, my Adorable Spouse": this is not betrothal but identification. And it is more than this too: not just His crucifixion but all others.

This excerpt belongs to an oft-cited portion of *Story of a Soul*, whose most famous passage spells out Thérèse's discontent:

> To be Your *Spouse*, to be a *Carmelite*, and by my union with You to be the *Mother* of souls, should not this suffice me? And yet it is not so. No doubt, these three privileges sum up my true *vocation*: *Carmelite*, *Spouse*, *Mother*, and yet I feel within me other vocations. I feel the vocation of the WARRIOR, THE PRIEST, THE APOSTLE, THE DOCTOR, THE MARTYR. Finally, I feel the need and the desire of carrying out the most heroic deeds for *You, O Jesus*. I feel within my soul the courage of the *Crusader*, the *Papal Guard*, and I would want to die on the field of battle in defense of the Church. (192, original emphasis)

Thérèse has drawn a gendered line here between the feminine roles she is permitted and the heroic vocations she yearns to inhabit, masculine roles in all caps. It is worth underscoring Thérèse's particular dissatisfaction with "my union with You": she has little interest in what will issue from the wedding she has announced. Wife, nun, mother: these do not suffice for a soul primed for battle.

It is difficult to imagine that Thérèse's Little Way could satisfy her desire for all and every kind, and yet it is precisely the folly of containing her dream, the disciplining of these fierce desires, that enables her shortcut to sainthood. In scaling great trials down to mundane privation, she attends to every irritation with the vehemence of a martyr. The rigors of this practice made Thérèse forbidding: when she recounts her efforts for the new entrants to Carmel, Thérèse acknowledges to the Prioress, "I know very well that your little lambs find me severe" (239). In thus confining herself to her given vocation, the profound unnaturalness of Thérèse's practice of devotion is not only the conversion of privation into privilege; it is the condition of a warrior shut into a cloister.

The continuation of the passage details further contortions:

> I feel in me the *vocation of* the PRIEST. With what love, O Jesus, I would carry You in my hands when, at my voice, You would come down from heaven. And with what love would I give You to souls! But alas! while desiring to be a *Priest*, I admire and envy the humility of St. Francis of Assisi and I feel the *vocation* of imitating him in refusing the sublime dignity of the *Priesthood*.
>
> O Jesus, my Love, my Life, how can I combine these contrasts? How can I realize the desires of my poor *little soul*? (192, original emphasis)

To feel the vocation to refuse the vocation that she feels: Thérèse's sainthood is constructed out of these straits. This built-in compunction to disable her own desire marks the deepest order of the unnatural; Thérèse's shortcut is a doubling back against herself. This passage asks the core question of *Story of a Soul* – "How can I realize the desires of my poor little soul? – and the answer is tortuous: to realize her desires, she must refuse them. This structure of reversal lays bare a black-and-white apparatus that advances her soul by impoverishing it – "poor little soul."

Thérèse wrote out the "story of her soul" and not her life; as Sackville-West notes, Thérèse is curiously silent about actual events at Lisieux.[43] The career of Thérèse's soul is the story of its diminishment into her Little Way; *Story of a Soul* is a record of Thérèse's dissatisfactions, all the way to the profound doubt that engulfed her soul during her last months. The childhood dream for all became a renunciation of little things in the cloister, but the miracle of Saint Thérèse is that her shortcut worked: though she did not "undergo all the tortures of the martyrs," she joined their ranks.

The model for Thérèse's most deeply felt longing is "dear sister" Joan of Arc. *Story of a Soul* recounts her childhood desire to imitate Joan of Arc, fueled by

---

[43] Sackville-West, *The Eagle and the Dove*, 125.

a God-given conviction that "I was born for *glory*": "He made me understand my own *glory* would not be evident to the eyes of mortals, that it would consist in becoming a great *saint!*" (72, original emphasis). Thérèse acted on her longing to imitate Joan of Arc at Lisieux, composing and producing two plays, *The Mission of Joan of Arc* and *Joan of Arc Accomplishes her Mission*, playing Joan in both. Mary Frohlich notes that Thérèse composed the first play in honor of the start of the official process of canonization for Joan of Arc by Pope Leo XIII in 1894 (90), which was achieved in 1920. Remarkably, Saint Thérèse of Lisieux was canonized in 1925, only five years after her medieval idol. So, though centuries separated them, they became sister saints of modern France.

"Erato / Love Poetry" enshrines Thérèse's performance as Joan of Arc: the opening photograph of the section features Thérèse in costume for her 1895 performance. The image in *Dictée* is less distinct than that featured in *Story of a Soul*, suggesting a xerographic softening. In the sharper photograph, we can discern the sword, standard, and shield, and *Story of a Soul* featured a magnified detail of Thérèse's form that features her dress overlayed with armor, as well as her flowing hair and fixed expression.[44] The detail image reveals Thérèse is looking away, into the distance, but in Cha's picture, she trains her gaze onto us. In *Dictée*, this image – like the others in the text – is uncaptioned; we can no longer make out the fleur-de-lys pattern on her dress and shield, and the sharpened points of her armor and weaponry are hazy whites. We see in *Dictée* a serious young woman bracing herself as she confronts us.

And so, though the moving picture of "Erato / Love Poetry" announces and depicts a marriage, its opening image presents not a bride but a martyr. This is not a movie about a union; it is a story of identification. The drama it stages is the identificatory process, dissected through the screen to emerge in the world. The montage across the pages of "Erato / Love Poetry" in fact cuts away the husband, whose human and divine incarnations are secondary to the more complex and passionate work of identification. The husband and the wife are givens, but "erato" is something more, as expressed in a single line from *Story of a Soul* that comprises an entire recto page: "The smallest act of PURE LOVE is of more value to her than all other works together" (115). We discover in *Story of a Soul* that Thérèse is recalling this line from Saint John of the Cross, and in citing it, she opens a further inquiry – "But is PURE LOVE in my heart?" – and then addresses the Bridegroom:

---

[44] Cha includes a full citation of *Story of a Soul* in *Dictée*'s notes, and the edition she used remains in print.

I feel, O Jesus, that after having aspired to the most lofty heights of Love, if one day I am not to attain them, I feel that I shall have tasted *more sweetness in my martyrdom and my folly* than I shall taste in the bosom of the *joy of the Fatherland*. (197, original emphasis)

Not the heights of love but the folly of her childhood dream of martyrdom; she deems the suffering sweeter than the reward.

"Erato / Love Poetry" is not about the union of husband and wife; it is about the identification of she and her, spectator and star, through the dream of martyrdom. The section closes with another performance of Joan of Arc, a close-up still from Carl Theodor Dreyer's 1928 film *The Passion of Joan of Arc*. Dreyer's film dramatized Joan's 1431 trial from transcripts of the proceedings, famously marrying historical fidelity to expressionistic aesthetic techniques. This sublime historical reenactment centers around the performance of Renée Falconetti, whose expression in Cha's still conveys a wearied understanding. This image is scrubbed of the beatific or tear-stained looks familiar to posters for the film: Joan's face is dry and her lips are parted, on the verge of speaking. I see this image as Cha's intended detail for the opening picture of Saint Thérèse of Lisieux: a close-up that insists upon an identity between two different actors, through their performances of the warrior saint.

I am reminded, too, of the advancing face of Spencer Brydon's alter ego in "The Jolly Corner": Brydon recalls the magic lantern, and in this film still I identify Cha's alter ego. Brydon fell before that face, but the concluding lines on the verso page of this closing portrait of Joan of Arc spells out a reversal: "her body all the time de composes / eclipses to be come yours" (118). The art of "Erato / Love Poetry" is the revelation of its apparatus, a machine of identification that merges spectator to star – as well as reader to author. Takada's telling characterization of the main thread of this section as "the fantasy enactment of the reader's relation to Cha's text" embeds a relation between the reader and Cha herself across these pages. Having traced the intertwining alter egos of "Erato / Love Poetry," I will conclude by returning to the author of *Dictée*.

Saint Theresa Hak Kyung Cha

Amid the prefatory material in *Dictée* is a sustained depiction of the experience of a Catholic mass: "Black ash from the Palm Hosannah. Ash. Kneel down on the marble the cold beneath rising through the bent knees. Close eyes and as the lids flutter, push out the tongue" (13). Cha attended Convent of the Sacred Heart, a Catholic French girls' school in the Bay Area, and she details ritual intertwined with study; the exercise of "Dictée" is embedded within these practices: "First Friday. One hour before mass. Mass every First Friday.

Dictée first. Every Friday. Before mass. Dictée before. Back in the study hall"
(18). The presentation of the mass features "He the one who becomes He" (13),
but the first translation exercise – "Dictée" – directs us to a different holy
personage:

> 1. Today would be the Feast day of the Immaculate Conception. She would
> have been voted to crown the Blessed Virgin. She herself would be sinless
> would be pure would be chaste in her heart. She would be silent. Often. Most
> of the time. Most often than not. Far too often. (14)

Later in this material, Cha depicts the process of entering into the chapel after
Dictée and specifies the crowning: "The chosen ones to crown Mary the
Immaculate Conception enter in the center" (19). The exercise, however,
offers a different process: not the chosen ones among the students but the
"she" who "would have been voted to crown the Blessed Virgin." In this
singular soul, I read Cha's longing as well as her self-perception: "Far too
often" silent.

"She herself would be sinless": this is a core conviction of *Dictée*, vital to its
apparatus of identification. This material works through a Catholic obsession
with sin: attending mass requires "the head of hair the sin covered" (13);
the second translation exercise recites the Catholic prayer of contrition ("I
detest all my sins"); the eighth demands, "Name all the sins." Upon completion
of these exercises, Cha takes us to confession: "Bless me father, for I have
sinned. My last confession was . . . I can't remember when . . . These are my
sins" (16). What follows is an italicized confession that transforms the ritual:
"*I am making up the sins. For the guarantee of absolution. In the beginning
again, at zero. Before Heaven even. Before the Fall. All previous wrongs erased.
Reduced to spotless. Pure. When I receive God, all pure*" (16–17, original
italics). Cha rewinds, veering away from the Catholic cosmology to found her
agency "at zero." *Dictée*'s governing ritual is a revised Catholicism free of sin.

As her confession continues, Cha details her "*Act of Contrition*": "*I am
making the confession. To make words. To make a speech in such tongues*"
(17, original italics). And she stands up to the confessor's challenge:

> *Q: WHO MADE THEE?*
> *A: God made me.*
> *To conspire in God's Tongue.*
> *Q: WHERE IS GOD?*
> *A: God is everywhere.*
> *Accomplice in His Texts, the fabrication in His Own Image, the pleas-*
> *ure the desire of giving Image to the word in the mind of the confessor.*
> (17, original italics)

As God's accomplice, she has charged herself with "giving Image to the word" – with a particular emphasis on "the pleasure the desire" of this labor. The confession builds to a concluding response that rivals Saint Thérèse's excesses:

> God who has made me in His own likeness. In His Own Image in His Own Resemblance, in His Own Copy, In His Own Counterfeit Presentment, in His Duplicate, in His Own Reproduction, in His Cast, in His Carbon, His Image and His Mirror. Pleasure in the image pleasure in the copy pleasure in the projection of likeness pleasure in the repetition. Acquiesce, to the correspondence. Acquiesce, to the messenger. Acquiesce, to and for the complot in the Hieratic tongue. Theirs. Into Their tongue, the counterscript, my confession in Theirs. Into Theirs. To scribe to make hear the words, to make sound the words, the words made flesh. (17–18, original italics)

This is Cha's confession, in which she spells out her ambition for her work. She claims her likeness to God, but on her terms, and the proliferating materials of reproduction – cast, carbon – recall her xerographic art and, more broadly, the techniques of the apparatus. We read the primary instigation for her identificatory work here – the founding condition that "God made me" – but in the pleasures she revels in, notably including the "pleasure in the projection of likeness," the artist takes part in the impetus reserved for the divine: Cha's powers of copying, of repetition, grant her the force of creation.

Yet this creative agency is the work of giving over: her confession, her "counterscript," is an acquiescence to Their tongue. *Dictée* is a product of this tension between the strictures and pleasures of creation, evident in the title that names the labor of composing "Into Their tongue." So, even as she raises her art to God's own "Counterfeit Presentment," the "correspondance" she achieves in claiming her own identity to God is a translation into terms that are not her own.[45] It is my contention, however, that Cha's purity and pleasure advance toward a condition that upends the "complot" that she was made to worship and study.

The passage concludes in the chapel, where the crowning of Mary launches the novena of the Immaculate Conception. Cha spells out the overlay of the Catholic novena and calls forth an epic beginning:

NOVENA: NINE EACH. THE RECITATION OF PRAYER AND PRACTICING OF DEVOTIONS DURING A NINE DAY PERIOD
And it begins. (19)

The nine chapters of *Dictée* correspond to a nine-day practice devoted to Mary. It is worth pointing out that the Feast Day of the Immaculate Conception does

---

[45] I am struck by the overtones of deconstruction in Cha's spelling of "correspondance."

not index Christ's conception. Instead, this celebration enshrines Mary's redemption: though she was born to human parents – or, to quote *Dictée*, "born of one mother and one father" (25) – Mary was redeemed at conception. Mary is sinless; she is full of grace, a pure vessel for holy parturition. In my reading of the first translation exercise, it is Cha who "would have been voted to crown the Blessed Virgin," and the correspondence in the "she" that follows ("She herself would be sinless would be pure would be chaste in her heart") installs the relation between "she" and "her" core to *Dictée* and particularly to the self-reflexive presentation of "Erato / Love Poetry."

The communion that matters is the play between Cha and the multiple shes of the text – and not "He the one who becomes He," who requires the ash and "Mea Culpa Mea Culpa through my most grievous sin" (13) that Cha depicts in the mass. Fashioned from the sinless redemption of Mary, the counterscript of *Dictée* frees itself from the strictures of sin. Saint Thérèse, too, appealed to the Blessed Virgin when she was gravely ill as a child, to experience an "ineffable grace" (66), Thérèse's practice of devotion significantly refuses the condemnation of sin. Her way is founded on a conviction that "He forgave me *in advance*"; indeed, "He *has forgiven* me not much but ALL" (83, 84, original emphasis). Her mortifications are not penance for sins but a series of identifications with the Savior. Cha's identification with Mary presents a crowning example of the inhabitation of women that runs through *Dictée*, and this novena conducts its devotions before her image: "the Holy Virgin Mary robed in blue with white drape or white robe with a blue drape over her head" (18).

"Of blue and white satin" (19): against all of the black and white of *Dictée* – every fabric and flower is white; blood and shadows are darkened to black – Mary's blue and white offers a different standard. Rather than the black and white of the apparatus, this is a guiding standard of purity and motherhood. The final day of *Dictée*'s novena, "Polymnia / Sacred Poetry," features a Korean myth of healing in which an unknown woman gives a child in search of medicine for her ailing mother a basket filled with special remedies.[46] Cha describes the woman's preparations: "She placed the white bowl in the center of the white cloth. The light renders each whiteness iridescent, encircling the bowl a purple hue" (169). I see in this emerging color a transcendence of the apparatus: "Polymnia / Sacred Poetry" tells its tale without the involuted meditations of the previous eight days of the novena. The child departs with the medicine:

---

[46] Sora Han's "Poetics of Mu," *Textual Practice* 34.6 (2020) reads the appearance of the Pari Gongju myth in *Dictée* in the context of Korea's postcolonial history.

> After a while she turned around to wave to the young woman at the well. She
> had already left the well. She turned and looked in all directions but she was
> not anywhere to be seen. (170)

These shes are not the becoming-other of "Erato / Love Poetry"; the child and
the woman need not change places. Instead, both are instantiations of Cha: the
woman at the well recalls the alter ego of "Erato," whose tears were displaced
onto "water dripping into the stone well"; the child acts on Cha's own yearning
to save her mother. This is a multiplication of subjects and not the transversal
operations between subject and object that risks both; this is the epic space of
myth in which woman and child can both be heroines.

   To be free from sin, however, is not to be free from suffering. Saint Thérèse
longed to suffer: to be Christ's bride did not suffice because she wanted to take
Christ's Passion, his divine suffering. Thérèse's mortifications were in the
service of self-exaltation, and she adhered to the standard of the warrior martyr
"born for glory." Neither *Story of a Soul* nor *Dictée* is a confession, and both
bear an oblique relation to autobiography, the genre born from the Christian
practice of penance. Both seek transcendence on battlefields of the soul, deep
interiors that threaten the integrity of the self. My ultimate claim is that *Dictée* is
a kind of hagiography that details not only the lives of saints but the suffering
entailed in embodying their lives.

   Dictée channels others through its central speaker, who suffers to inhabit the
experience of historical, mythic, and familial others; this is a hagiography
overwritten by the feeling act of presenting these lives. The fifth translation
exercise of the *Dictée* embedded in the Catholic mass conveys the urgency of
this work; amid the exercises, laden with information, emerges a broken
English:

> She call she believe she calling to she has calling because there no response
> she believe she calling and the other end must hear. The other end must see
> the other end feel
> she accept pages sent care of never to be seen never to be read never to be
> known if name if name be known if name only seen heard spoken read cannot
> be never she hide all essential words words link subject verb she writes
> hidden the essential words must be pretended invented she try on different
> images essential invisible (15)

This is a rendering of the call the diseuse answers; this is her vocation. She
accepts what "the other end must see" and "feel" on pages that contain "essential words." I am struck by "writes" – the only standard verb conjugation in the
passage: we recognize Cha's voice at this point, gathered from an immigrant
English.

To "try on different images" is the work of *Dictée*, which revives martyrs. The reward for Christian martyrdom is the remission of all sin, but the crucial qualification of sinlessness renders Cha herself "Before Heaven even. Before the Fall." Like Mary, she is redeemed before acts of parturition, but without the trappings of heaven and original sin, there is "No end in sight" (140). The later portions of *Dictée* ponder the decision "to take the call" (139) that led to an "extended journey, horizontal in form, in concept" (150). This is a movement into and out of death without the promise of ascension – only suffering.

Dictée opens with its diseuse in the agony of bringing forth others: "Swallows with last efforts last wills against the pain that wishes it to speak" (3). She is pregnant with the speech of others – "All barren cavities to make swollen. The others each occupying her" (3) – and the passage concludes with "The delivery" (5). Like Mary, the diseuse is charged with delivering martyrs, but Cha's sinlessness, detached from redemption, floods its pleasures – in the image, the copy, the projection – with the pain of delivery. In taking on this pain, the diseuse is herself a martyr. She traverses a way laden with agony, whose stations have been unmoored from the eschatological telos of Saint Thérèse's Tomorrow.

Thérèse was no more assured as she suffered through the final stages of tuberculosis. Saints' deaths determine their lives, and Saint Thérèse's is the telos to the story of her soul. The Epilogue to *Story of a Soul* explains that Thérèse put down her pen three months before her death and then describes this unwritten portion of her life. Thérèse soldiered on through months of physical agony, but she was a martyr who had lost her cause. On the day of her death, before her three sisters, "Thérèse pointed to the statue of the Blessed Virgin and said to them: '*Oh! I prayed fervently to her! But it is pure agony; there is no consolation!*'" (269, original italics). As the afternoon wore on, Thérèse reassured her sisters in attendance that "*To die of love does not mean to die in transports*" (269, original italics), and her famous final words offer a recuperation: "*My God, I love you!*" (271, original italics). But I am left with the trial of Thérèse's soul, the agony of her dream of martyrdom.

Cathy Park Hong's portrait of Theresa Hak Kyung Cha in *Minor Feelings* builds toward a revelation by Cha's brother John. After Cha's death, their mother dreamed that "Cha was a little girl who led her to a number, 710" and "her sister Bernadette also had a vision of three 7s" (177). When New York City police failed to locate Cha's missing belongings, John, with another brother, James, and Cha's widower, Richard, conducted their own search: "They came to a stairway that led to three white brick columns marked with the numbers 710, 711, and 713, which stopped John in his tracks," leading them to search the vicinity, where they found her gloves, "puffed up as if there were invisible hands inside them." For John, this vision is his sister's "final art piece" – but Hong records her misgivings about his story: "I was spellbound when he told me his account. But afterwards, I grappled with whether or not to include John's story, since it cloaked Cha back in that shroud" (178). It seems to me, however, that as this story shrouds, it also extends Cha's work into other lives.

Hong goes over the "trick" of grief, which "can bend our perceptions to reassure us that our lost loved ones are near:

> Of course, their minds will insist that she's still present, leading them to the room, the energy of her hands still in the gloves, in their dreams, in *Dictée*, calling from the underworld. (178)

I am struck by Hong's inclusion of *Dictée* in her litany of the places that retain Cha's energy. The progression from the gloves to the dreams of Cha's family and then to *Dictée* maps out a growing field for her energy, "calling from the underworld." The presence of the author in her text, of course, is not a product of grief; it is the particular force of *Dictée* to lay bare Theresa Hak Kyung Cha, who calls to us from a web of interactions that span familial, national, and literary histories.

When we read *Dictée*, we encounter its brutalized author. In its images of underground souls, tortured political prisoners, and Catholic martyrs, we feel the reverberating passion of Theresa Hak Kyung Cha. Saint Thérèse of Lisieux is my guide for comprehending Cha's martyrdom: Thérèse Martin's life ended in an agony that devastated her dream of suffering; Cha's rape and murder plummets her diseuse far below the deepest recesses of the text, shattering the hollow bowl of its underworld. But though Thérèse did not die in transports, the raising of her ghost fast-tracked her to sainthood. Theresa Hak Kyung Cha's ghost lingered in the aftermath of her demise, to pervade the dreams of her family; she lives still, in *Dictée*, to haunt her readers.

Envoi

I close with a poem by Cha's sister Bernadette presented in the afterword to *The Dream of the Audience*, the exhibition catalogue for the major retrospective of Theresa Hak Kyung Cha's work at the Berkeley Art Museum in 2001. It begins with a call to her sister – "Hak Kyung Hak Kyung" – and an explanation for Bernadette's silence "Until now":

> Any reference to you
> Would surely cause the words that would form upon my lips to unravel
> Would isolate me would separate me from your existence
> Your memory your silence within my blood[47]

---

[47] Bernadette Cha, Afterword, in *The Dream of the Audience*, 51.

The shared blood flows in the style and tone of these lines, so reminiscent of her sister's art. Bernadette, a collaborator and frequent subject for her sister's work, has been a guardian of her silence. On the occasion of this exhibit, nearly twenty years after Cha's death, Bernadette risks separating herself by presenting her memories:

I recall.
She, no larger than I, carried me on her back.[48]

This "she" bears the fact of separation, from the "you" of the poem's second-person address to the third person who inhabits her memory. From this distinction, Bernadette can sense and admire the sister who carried her: "She was strong." More memories emerge:

I recall.
She lay there in a polished wooden box.
We chose pine.
It was quiet.
The sun was shining upon her hands.
She was silent.
I spoke to her anyway.[49]

As Bernadette's memories resolve into images, they lose the traces of her sister's voice. These lines are bereft of Cha's "Sapphic shrapnel," presenting instead Bernadette's quiet vigil.

The poem concludes with a final memory and an envoi:

I recall.
Our shadows cast on white, translucent curtains.
She, winding yarn into a large ball pulling the line from my circling arms as I watched
The last bit of it fall from my hand and inch across the floor, then onto her lap vanishing
      into her hands.
Jhal – ga Uhn-ni[50]

I am reminded of Thérèse's childhood memory, in which her sister Céline chose a ball of yarn and Thérèse took the entire basket. Saint Thérèse wanted all; Theresa Hak Kyung Cha wound the yarn so it disappeared into her hands: Cha's art, which pulls in threads. Bernadette's repeated emphasis on Cha's hands recalls, too, John's vision of her gloves "puffed up, as if there were invisible hands inside them" (178). The faith that ventures into invisible realms is a living love.

The final line, in Korean, translates to "go well, big sister." Here is the return of the second person, rendered in the language of Hak Kyung and

[48] Ibid., 53.   [49] Ibid., 53.   [50] Ibid., 54.

Hak Eun – Bernadette's Korean name, appended at the close of her afterword. This intimacy cuts against the public-facing materials of the exhibition: Bernadette can finally bid her lost sister good-bye in the presence of her art, all made by hands with a trick for vanishing. She finally sends off her sister here, where her presence is everywhere.

Theresa Hak Kyung Cha in Black and White has sought to uncover a mechanism for writing the self in the work of *Dictée*. From the identificatory processes revealed in the flicker of the cinematic apparatus, this study has been an inquiry into the literary dimensions of Cha's art. Tracing autographical intertexts into her masterwork, I have arrived at the death of Theresa Hak Kyung Cha, recorded in black and white.

References

Alvergue, José Felipe. "Poetic Seeing / Beyond Telling: The 'Call' in Theresa Hak Kyung Cha's *Dictée*." *College Literature* 43.2 (2016): 427–456.

Barthes, Roland. "Upon Leaving the Movie Theater." *Apparatus. Cinematographic Apparatus: Selected Writings*. Ed. Theresa Hak Kyung Cha. New York: Tanam Press, 1981. 1–4.

Baudry, Jean-Louis. "The Apparatus." *Apparatus. Cinematographic Apparatus: Selected Writings*. Ed. Theresa Hak Kyung Cha. New York: Tanam Press, 1981. 41–62.

Baudry, Jean-Louis. "Author and Analyzable Subject." *Apparatus. Cinematographic Apparatus: Selected Writings*. Ed. Theresa Hak Kyung Cha. New York: Tanam Press, 1981. 67–83.

Bro, Father Bernard. *Saint Thérèse of Lisieux: Her Family, Her God, Her Message*. San Francisco: Ignatius Press, 2003.

Cha, Bernadette. "Afterword." *The Dream of the Audience: Theresa Hak Kyung Cha (1951–1982)*. Ed. Constance M. Lewallen. Berkeley: University of California Press, 2001. 51–55.

Cha, Theresa Hak Kyung, ed. *Apparatus. Cinematographic Apparatus: Selected Writings*. New York: Tanam Press, 1981.

Cha, Theresa Hak Kyung. *Dictée*. Berkeley, CA: Third Woman Press, 1995.

Cheng, Anne Anlin. *The Melancholy of Race: Psychoanalysis, Assimilation, and Hidden Grief*. New York: Oxford University Press, 2000.

Craig, Eleanor. "The Ambiguity of Devotion: Complicity and Resistance in Theresa Hak Kyung Cha's *DICTÉE*." *Representations* 153 (2021): 85–104.

Fanon, Frantz. *Black Skin White Masks*. New York: Grove Press, 1967.

Fraser, Alison. "Diasporic Object Lessons: Material Identity and the Korean Diaspora in the Work of Theresa Hak Kyung Cha." *Women's Studies Quarterly* 47.1&2 (2019): 31–47.

Frohlich, Mary. "Introduction." *St. Thérèse of Lisieux: Essential Writings*. Ed. Frohlich. Maryknoll, NY: Orbis Books, 2003. 13–31.

Gaucher, Guy. *The Passion of Thérèse of Lisieux*. New York: Crossroad, 1998.

Han, Sora. "Poetics of Mu," *Textual Practice* 34.6 (2020): 921–948.

Hong, Cathy Park. *Minor Feelings: An Asian American Reckoning*. New York: One World – Random House, 2020.

Inoue, Mayumo. "Theresa Hak Kyung Cha's 'Phantomnation': Cinematic Specters and Spectral Collectivity in *Dictée* and *Apparatus*." *Criticism* 56.1 (2014): 63–87.

James, Henry. "The Jolly Corner." *Ghost Stories of Henry James*. Ware, Hertfordshire: Wordsworth Editions, 2001. 306–334.

Jeon, Joseph Jonghyun. *Racial Things, Racial Forms: Objecthood in Avant-Garde Asian American Poetry*. Iowa City: University of Iowa Press, 2012.

Kim, Hyo. "Embodying the In-Between: Theresa Hak Kyung Cha's *Dictée*." *Mosaic* 46.4 (2013): 127–143.

Kim, Sue J. "*Apparatus*: Theresa Hak Kyung Cha and the Politics of Form." *Journal of Asian American Studies* 8.2 (2005): 143–169.

Phu, Thy. "Decapitated Forms: Theresa Hak Kyung Cha's Visual Text and the Politics of Visibility." *Mosaic* 38.1 (2005): 17–36.

Sackville-West, Vita. *The Eagle and the Dove: A Study in Contrasts*. London: Michael Joseph, 1943.

Schiebe, Mark. "Stereo Rivalry in James's 'The Jolly Corner.'" *American Literary Realism* 50.1 (2017): 49–62.

Spahr, Juliana. "Postmodernism, Readers, and Theresa Hak Kyung Cha's *DICTÉE*." *College Literature* 23.3 (1996): 22–43.

Takada, Mayumi. "Annihilating Possibilities: Witnessing and Testimony through Cinematic Love in Theresa Hak Kyung Cha's *Dictée*." *Literature Interpretation Theory* 17 (2006): 23–48.

Thompson, Terry. "That 'Beautiful Art': Black-and-White Photography in Henry James's 'The Jolly Corner.'" *Interdisciplinary Literary Studies* 18.3 (2016): 395–412.

Thérèse, de Lisieux, Saint. *Story of a Soul: The Autobiography of St. Thérèse of Lisieux*. Washington, DC: Institute of Carmelite Studies, 2017.

Trinh T. Minh-ha. "White Spring." *The Dream of the Audience: Theresa Hak Kyung Cha (1951–1982)*. Ed. Constance M. Lewallen. Berkeley: University of California Press, 2001. 33–49.

Vernet, Marc. "Blinking, Flickering, and Flashing of the Black-and-White Film." *Apparatus. Cinematographic Apparatus: Selected Writings*. Ed. Theresa Hak Kyung Cha. New York: Tanam Press, 1981. 357–369.

Cambridge Elements ☰

Poetry and Poetics

Eric Falci
University of California, Berkeley

Eric Falci is Professor of English at the University of California–Berkeley. He is the author of *Continuity and Change in Irish Poetry, 1966–2010* (2012), *The Cambridge Introduction to British Poetry, 1945–2010* (2015), and *The Value of Poetry* (2020). With Paige Reynolds, he is the co-editor of *Irish Literature in Transition, 1980–2020* (2020). His first book of poetry, *Late along the Edgelands*, appeared in 2019.

About the Series
Cambridge Elements in Poetry and Poetics features expert accounts of poetry and poets across a broad field of historical periods, national and transnational traditions, linguistic and cultural contexts, and methodological approaches. Each volume offers distinctive approaches to poems, poets, institutions, concepts, and cultural conditions that have shaped the histories of poetic making.

Cambridge Elements ≡

Poetry and Poetics

Elements in the Series

Printed in the United States
by Baker & Taylor Publisher Services